The Scientific Method

The Scientific Method

Poems by Kim Roberts

WordTech Editions

© 2017 by Kim Roberts

Published by WordTech Editions
P.O. Box 541106
Cincinnati, OH 45254-1106

ISBN: 9781625492166

Poetry Editor: Kevin Walzer
Business Editor: Lori Jareo

Visit us on the web at www.wordtechweb.com

Cover design by Dan Vera

Cover photo: "Fred Ott's Sneeze," Edison Kinetoscope, William K.L. Dickinson, 1894

for my big brother,
Dr. Kenneth Berwick Roberts

Acknowledgments

For their invaluable advice and support, I thank Abigail Beckel, Regie Cabico, Teri Ellen Cross Davis, Christina Daub, Michael Gushue, Elizabeth Poliner, and Dan Vera.

Thanks also to the following artist retreats, where some of these poems were written: The Artist at Pine Needles Fellowship at the St. Croix Watershed Research Station; The Edward Albee Foundation; Hambidge Center for the Arts; Kimmel-Harding-Nelson Center for the Arts; The Mesa Refuge; Millay Colony for the Arts; New York Mills Arts Retreat; Soul Mountain Retreat; and the Virginia Center for the Creative Arts.

My gratitude to the editors of the following journals and anthologies where these poems first appeared, sometimes in earlier versions:

Journals:
Ascent: "Walt Whitman's Brain"; *Barrelhouse*: "Nikola Tesla"; *Beloit Poetry Journal*: "The International Fruit of Welcome"; *Blue Lyra Review*: "The Invasive Weed Syndicate"; *The Broadkill Review*: "The News"; *Burnt District*: "Caseus"; *Calliope*: "Photo with Woman at Clothes Line"; *District Lit*: "Turkey in the Straw" and "Thirteen Ways of Looking at DC Not Endorsed by the Tourist Board"; *Gargoyle*: "The Thing in the Thing" and "Half-Built House"; *The Ilanot Review* (Israel): "The Vital Force"; *Innisfree Poetry Journal*: "Botany"; *Jabberwock Review*: "In the Village"; *Junctures: The Journal for Thematic Dialogue* (New Zealand): "The Shipwreck"; *Little Patuxent Review*: "Protandric"; *Mickle Street Review*: "Walt Whitman's Brain," "American Herring Gull," and "Fowler and Wells' Phrenological Cabinet"; *Mi Poesias*: "Life in Connecticut, October 1704: From the Journal of Sarah Kemble Knight"; *Northern Virginia Review*: "After Hours in the Kindergarten"; *Open Letters*: "Moons of Grief"; *Poemelion*: "Van Gogh at Arles"; *Poor Yorick*: "The Cardiff Giant"; *Re)Verb*: "Radiolaria"; *Theodate*: "The Garden of Ryoan-ji"; *Truck*: "Sonnet for the U.S. Capitol Dome"; *Unsplendid*: "Hearing Loss"; *Up the Staircase Quarterly*: "E Pluribus Unum"; *Virginia Quarterly Review*, "Double Indemnity"; *Wallace Stevens Journal*: "Mystery Piano in the Woods"; and *The Wide Shore*: "Carl Sagan's Turtleneck Sweater."

Anthologies:
Capitals, Bloomsbury Publishing, 2016: "Swamp"; *Resisting Arrest: Poems to Stretch the Sky,* Jacar Press, 2016: "Campaign Speech, 1896: 'The Scourge of Foreign Elements'"; *The Crafty Poet II,* Terrapin Books, 2016: "Six"; *Joys of the Table,* Richer Resources Publications, 2015: "International Fruit of Welcome"; *The Southern Poetry Anthology, Vol. VII: North Carolina,* Texas Review Press, 2015: "Invasive Weed Syndicate"; *Lavandaria: A Mixed Load of Woman, Wash and Word,* San Diego City Works Press, 2009: "Photo with Woman at Clothes Line"; *Letters to the World: Poems from the WOM-PO Listserv,* Red Hen Press, 2008: "Fowler and Wells' Phrenological Cabinet"; *Poetic Voices Without Borders 2,* Gival Press, 2008: "Radiolaria"; *DC Poets Against the War: An Anthology,* Argonne House, 2004: "In the Village."

Reprints and Special Projects:
"American Herring Gull" was reprinted in *Huntington Literary Quarterly,* December 2010 and *Global Waters Magazine,* USAID, 2012. It was also reprinted in "The Poetics of Water," the exhibition catalogue for an exhibit by the Take Me To The River arts collective, University of Maryland College Gallery, 2011. The Goethe-Institut of Washington published an excerpt of "Swamp" in three languages (English, German, and Mandarin) on a limited edition poster for their 2009 Time Shadows series. The poem also appeared in three languages in its entirety on their website. *Redux Literary Journal* reprinted "Radiolaria" and "Nikola Tesla" in 2012, and "The Shipwreck," "The Thing in the Thing" and "After Hours in the Kindergarten" in 2015. *Verse Daily* reprinted "The International Fruit of Welcome" in 2012. *Wordgathering* reprinted "Hearing Loss" in 2014. Split This Rock reprinted "Protandric" in *The Quarry* in 2015; "The Thing in the Thing" was reprinted in the Association of Jewish Libraries 2015 Jubilee Conference Proceedings. "Caseus" and "Selenium" were included in "EAT: A Literature Photography Installation" at Centre College, Danville, KY, 2016.

Table of Contents

I.

The Scientific Method..13
The Thing in the Thing..15
The Invasive Weed Syndicate.....................................16
Caseus...17
Protandric...18
Botany...19
In Memoriam: Ming the Clam....................................20
Moons of Grief..21
Fowler and Wells' Phrenological Cabinet.................22
The Moon and *The Sun*..24
Abandoned Constellations..26
Immunity..28
Walt Whitman's Brain..29
Nikola Tesla...30
Building the Perhapsitron...31
Carl Sagan's Turtleneck Sweater................................32
"Fred Ott's Sneeze"...33
Sucker Rods...34
The Bluebonnet Carries 2,000 Amps.........................35
The Cardiff Giant..37
The News..38

II.

Hatchery...41
A Boy Named Schmutz..43
In the Village...44
Vilna..45
Radiolaria...46
The Vital Force..48
Sabbath...49

Campaign Speech, 1896: "The Scourge of Foreign
  Elements"..50
Selenium..51
Burbot..52
Life in Connecticut, October 1704: From the Journal of
  Sarah Kemble Knight...53
I am the Pâtissier of God...54
Turkey in the Straw..55
Hearing Loss..56
Six...57
The Immovable Empyrean..58
The International Fruit of Welcome............................60

III.
Swamp..63
Sonnet for the U.S. Capitol Dome................................64
Presidential Rondeaux..65
E Pluribus Unum...67
Quebec Place NW, Park View Neighborhood............68
After Hours in the Kindergarten..................................70
Double Indemnity...71
Extreme Makeover: The Home Edition......................73
Photo with Woman at Clothes Line.............................74
Thirteen Ways of Looking at DC Not Endorsed by the
  Tourist Board..75
Mystery Piano in the Woods...76
The Garden of Ryoan-Ji...77
The Shipwreck...78
The Suicide of Clover Adams..79
Half-Built House...82
Van Gogh at Arles...83
The Glass Flowers at Harvard.......................................84
American Herring Gull..86

Notes..89

I.

The Scientific Method

Thomas Alva Edison's Laboratory Complex, West Orange, NJ

1. Chemistry Laboratory

Test tubes and retorts, powders
in stoppered bottles, some bright blue.
Chemistry proceeds in increments,
we try this, fail, try that.

From stoppered bottles, some bright blue
powder of nickel citrate
—try this, wrong amount. Try that:
the pure color of a robin's egg.

Powder of nickel citrate
waits to reveal its secrets.
The colors, burnt orange, robin's egg,
bloom in the high-pressure distill.

To reveal a thing's secrets,
patience and precision are required.
To bloom in a high-pressure distill
demands just the smallest change.

Patience and repetition are required.
Watch your test tubes and retorts, your powders,
for just the smallest change, proof
of how chemistry proceeds. In increments.

2. Stockroom

The new supplies have just arrived.
Rhinoceros horn and elephant hide
catalogued and shelved, wait mutely
for some mucker to decide
that their covalent dipeptide
might serve some unaccustomed duty.

When blizzards locked two men inside
Fessenden and Ayls survived
three days on items picked astutely
from the new supplies.

Wayward innovation thrives
as muckers wander down the aisles
buggered by the absolutely
varied proofs of worldly beauty
fresh applications might devise.
Eccentric fancy is their guide
through the new supplies.

The Thing in the Thing

Is the chimney a chute of air where grey smoke
clots and rises? Or is the chimney the bricks,

the mason's careful art? Is the car a box of metal,
a web of gauges and fuses, or the feeling of speed

gathering under your right foot? The tree waves its branches
and becomes, thanks to wind, more tree. The clouds

lend more meaning to the sky. Water maintains
its fluidity even while held in the confines of a glass:

a glass of water is a shape, not a nature. The true nature
of a thing, its essence, is something pure and focused

like a stone holding its hardness. A telephone holds its ring
as pure potentiality. Then it does ring, and it's Gwen,

and she's telling me a story about her sister in Knoxville,
or explaining the common root of a word in Italian

and a word in Hebrew. Not knowing the name of a thing
changes nothing, but when I can,

I like to know. The sky holds nothing back. Every time
the barometer drops, it makes some big confession.

The Invasive Weed Syndicate

Shepherd's Purse

A rude ring of lobed leaves clings
to the bottom of the stem, and from this stage
the actors rise in heart-shaped pods
and strip to white petticoats by the open road.

Bull Thistle

A ratchety stem with spiny leaves splays;
at the top of each spear, a green gumdrop
garbed in angry spikes wears a hot pink mohawk,
and the bees hone in and get drunk.

Chickweed

Tight oval buds covered in a coarse white beard
pop open to reveal a tiny white flower
like a loose corona following the sun.
Little prospector: beware the claim jumper.

Fleabane

Leaves like elongated spoons climb,
alternating, left and right, as if marching
in single file. The buds droop at the top
as if from shame. So much
is beyond our control.

Nutgrass

Tri-corner stems shoot from underground tubers,
a deep blackish-red, that tunnel
under the crops. This mission is a go:
pulling them up leaves the nutlets behind,
pulling them just makes it worse.

Caseus

> *How can anyone be expected to govern a country with 325 cheeses?"*—Charles de Gaulle

Caesar ate his first blue cheese
just west of Rocquefort,
in the town of Saint-Affrique.
In Latin it was *caseus*,
which became *cacio* in Italian,
queso in Spanish, *queijo*
in Portuguese. Cheese.
The Roman farmer Columella
described how to get rennet
from the fourth stomach
of a lamb, how to add it
to fresh milk, how long to wait
for the milk to curdle,
how to press the whey out,
how to salt the curds until dry.
In *The Odyssey*, the Cyclops
drained his curds in wicker baskets
lining the walls of his cave.
The baskets gave the cheese
its form—in Greek *formos*—
in Italian *formaggio*, in French
fromage. Virgil ate fresh cheese
with chestnuts. The techniques
of ripening and airing, *affinage*,
are secrets passed down
thousands of years. Right now,
in some cave in France,
a farmer is carefully turning
each wheel, salting one side,
watching the mold emerge.

Protandric

Oysters may look to us
like wet floppy tongues,

but there's no licking.
There's no touching.

Oysters are *protandric*—
they can change sex at will.

All oysters are born male.
They change to female

the following season.
They seem to like being female

most of the time. The older the oyster,
the more likely he'll be female.

And you thought
they were an aphrodisiac?

One male ejaculates
then every male in the colony

follows suit. Soon the waves
look like milk. The eggs

sway like belly dancers. It's spring!
Once again, it's spring.

Botany

Soft dusk creeps up my window sill and perches there, a little bird.

It is the moment of turning on the lights. *Troubles are like birds: they can fly.*

The Rose family has many turnings: it includes almond trees, strawberries, apples. Kinship is a funny thing.

Who would have thought an apple was cousin to a rose? It is the moment of turning on lights, but I haven't yet, watching the sky purple.

I am watching the shadows climb the pages of my open book, where an apple tree blossoms. Apples—"American as apple pie"—are native to Asia and Africa.

The fruit of the tree of knowledge in Genesis was not an apple, as I was taught. Botanists believe it was an apricot. *Troubles are like birds: they can fly.* I am dreaming idly of family.

I am dreaming about my family, holding my botany book open. This is what they say in parts of East Africa, about kin: *Troubles are like birds.* The book resembles two pale wings against a royal sky.

In Memoriam: Ming the Clam
(1499 – 2006)

The oldest known living
animal, Ming
was dredged up
still alive, age 507,
off Iceland.

Sclerochronologists
can count the rings
on their shells the same way
dendrochronologists
study tree rings.

The ocean quahog
or *arctica islandica*
lives in the top two inches
of muddy substrates
off the freezing coasts

of northern Europe
and North America.
Climate, sea temperature,
food supply—all
the environmental changes

are embedded there,
coated in a tough black
periostracum.
Inside her shell,
Ming shone like the moon.

Moons of Grief

There are moons that orbit Grief;
they are, finally, an escape off
    that sorry planet.
The moons are dumpy and irregular
and resemble
    rotating potatoes
but they are beautiful in their scarred, pocked,
imperfect way,
    turning on their elliptic
through roaring blackness.
When you finally reach
    the moon
that you'll make yours, named
after the Roman
    God of Sadness,
that view of the distant planet
wrapped in veils of cloud
    will seem a comfort,
although for a long while you'll still describe it
as one might describe
    a wound.

Fowler and Wells' Phrenological Cabinet

Walt Whitman made regular visits.
        He loved to touch the white porcelain head,
marked off in sections: Appetite, Grief,
Acquisitiveness. Like a butcher's chart

mapping the choicest meats.
        Whitman knew the body's limits,
and how the mind, a grid
of memory and fear, narrows the range

even further. He hated limits,
        prudence, high manners,
but he loved a good system
and wanted to learn this one's

steady answers. Why wouldn't
        what's inside show up on the skin?
The bumps of the head,
Small ones like hiccups,

Large ones that span three or four
        categories, elongated heads, ones
that come to a point. His categories
would need new names:

Voluptuousness wears an open collar,
        Indolence takes the shape
of a cardboard butterfly perched
on his finger. Adhesiveness wants a walk

on the dark docks, a ferry ride across the river.
        And Sublimity roars like a leaf.
His home in Camden,
where I touched his rubber galoshes,

once overflowed with stacks of paper,
        a chaos, a fire hazard.
He wouldn't let the hired woman touch it.
Whitman claimed an internal logic

even to Disorder; he loved
        a good system. In the prison
across the street from his house, men
line the windows.

Their wives and girlfriends
        dance on the sidewalk,
arms above their heads,
hold a pose like Cleopatra,

then change.
        I thought at first: performance art?
Then realized they were spelling
with their bodies, forming M

and Y and P in the air.
        The body's news comes slowly.
Whitman knew about longing,
he nursed dying Civil War soldiers,

knew the stink of rotting flesh,
        pus staining a bandage yellow,
the angel face we wear when we're asleep.
He was large in Sympathy.

He knew something of fate
        and its strange journey through the gray
thickets of Infelicity and Melancholia,
the temperaments that form in the womb.

The Moon and *The Sun*

In 1836, *The New York Sun* reported
Sir John Herschel, the celebrated astronomer,
had built a telescope "of vast dimensions
and entirely new principle" and discovered

on the moon a race of flying men
with wings like bats. They worshipped
in sapphire temples among basaltic hills
and lived in peace with a species

of tailless beaver, blue goats, and other
exotic fauna. The man-bats were covered
in glossy, copper-colored hair
and attained a height of four feet.

Herschel called them *Vespertilio-homo*;
he said "some of their amusements
would ill comport with terrestrial
notions of decorum" but they engaged

in what appeared animated conversation,
collected fruit, and bathed
in lunar rivers in the company
of spherical amphibious roly-polies.

All New York rang with the discoveries,
newsboys yelled out headlines,
every parlor hosted avid debates,
the story was reprinted in papers as far

as Cincinnati, lithographs were published,
a children's book, a play.
With their new steam-power presses
they printed tens of thousands of copies,

a penny apiece; "our only present difficulty
is to strike off sufficient number"
to meet demand. They printed
six articles on six stunning days.

Some called it mere moonshine,
but *The Sun* never wavered. "We do not
hesitate to say that our enormous circulation
is the greatest of any daily paper."

The Sun printed "certificates of credence"
to ward off skeptics whose "consummate ignorance
is always incredulous to the higher order
of scientific discoveries."

Abandoned Constellations

Some disappeared as Earth
grew brighter. Some just fell out of favor.
Some were mere flattery:

Louis XIV's hand and scepter
(proposed by the royal astronomer)
or the crossed swords of Saxony

to honor the German Emperor Leopold.
My favorites among the obsolete
showed off the new technologies,

as if their invention were star-prophesied.
Tubus Herschelii Major,
Sir William Herschel's largest telescope,

Machina Electrica, stars forming
the cube of an electric generator.
Or the crowded chaos

of *Officina Typographica*, the printing office.
In the 1801 star atlas *Uranographia*,
it jobbed up east of Sirius. Did its noise

keep the neighbors up at night?
Did *Canis Minor* bark for hours?
And little *Pyxis Nautica*,

the Mariner's Compass: did the printer
interrupt its navigation, confusing
its ascension and declination,

pulling barques and schooners
wildly off their course?
Retired rollers and plate cylinders

clang no more. *Monoceros*,
the unicorn, lives atop those same stars,
straddles the press with its hind legs.

The stern of *Argo Navis* covers
the box of movable type. This section
of the celestial sphere,

previously gerrymandered
by Johann Bode, has returned
to form. Held in place

by frisket and tympan,
the inky sky fades back to black.
No characters, no ligatures,

no copyright, no authorship.
Gutenberg stands mute.
Silence reigns in space once more.

Immunity

I don't really understand T-cells
but when my doctor describes them,
I imagine Ts posted at intervals
in my bloodstream, like sentries
at a crenellated wall.
Are they T-shaped?
Or is T merely the first initial
of a long, inscrutable, Latin word?
I see a line of cells holding shields
emblazoned with Ts.
I hear their rhythmic chant,
T - T - T - T - T,
as they fall into formation
for their regular bloodstream drills.

Walt Whitman's Brain

Removed despite his brother's objections,
the brain was placed in an oil-cloth bag
and ferried across the Delaware River
to the American Anthropometric Society

in Philadelphia. One doctor noted
the "magnificent symmetry of the skull"
and recorded a 45-ounce weight.
The autopsy states it would join

a collection of "high-type brains"
of scientists and eminent men.
Injected with a special solution,
the brain would be hardened and preserved,

the external surfaces photographed,
and a plaster cast made. The brain
could then be compared with lesser types:
apes and criminals and women.

But none of this was done. When the brain
was accidentally dropped, it broke up, it ran:
each component part that Whitman believed
corresponded to a personality trait

dispersed, Self-esteem dribbling down
the examination table, Caution skidding
behind the door, Adhesiveness splashed
on the doctor's hands, Combativeness lurking

by the legs of a wooden stool, Philoprogenitiveness
in lumps on the lab's white tile floor.
The oily scum of the preserving alcohol,
The stench, the dashed and sticky remnants.

Nikola Tesla

Memorized entire books as a teenager in Serbia.
Arrived in the US with a letter of introduction to Edison,
dug ditches until he could open his own lab.

Developed the first motor for alternating current,
and lit the World's Fair in Chicago.
Believed chastity helped build a scientific mind.

Held the first radio patent and made early discoveries
in robotics. Heard radio chatter
from Venus and Mars. Fluent in eight languages.

Ate only boiled vegetables
whose cubic footage he could estimate
at a glance. Hated fat people.

Needed three napkins when eating;
walked around buildings three times before entering;
stayed in hotel rooms with numbers

divisible by three. Built a "death ray"
no government would buy.
Harnessed Niagara Falls for electrical power.

Afraid to touch anything round.
Afraid to touch human hair other than his own.
Afraid of squares of paper dropped into bowls of water.

Physically revolted by jewelry, especially pearl earrings.
Adored pigeons and nursed injured ones
in his hotel room.

Lived his last ten years in Room 3327
of the Hotel New Yorker.
Died in debt.

Building the Perhapsitron

He once said after the first billion
no one is going to stop us.

A synthetic star is a cryptic marvel:
the magnetic fields are invisible,
the plasma makes no sound.
In a vacuum chamber, a super-hot
cloud of heavy hydrogen
will rotate faster than the speed of sound.

He built a concrete bunker,
nearly the shape of a cube.
Physicists coined a nomenclature
for the instabilities: sawteeth, drift,
counterstreaming, sausage,
tearing, bump-in-tail, helical kink.

The history of physics is littered
with unrealized outcomes:
half-built machinery packed in crates,
excavated earth filled with pooling rainwater.
The triumphant announcement,
followed by scientific retreat
and humiliation, set a pattern
that would plague the field for decades.

Back in Aspen, he went up the chairlifts
again and again, and turned the idea over.
They gave him time off from his work
on the hydrogen bomb to set up a secret
thermonuclear project in an old rabbit hutch.

Carl Sagan's Turtleneck Sweater

They've got Carl Sagan's turtleneck sweater
in a vitrine in the lobby of the National
Geographic auditorium. *Did you see it?*
It's completely 70s; just perfect, Dan
reports. I think: someone manufactured

billions and billions of dated turtlenecks,
but that's what Dan likes
about this display; it's so modest
and ordinary. It doesn't shout
Express that in parsecs.

Imagine touching Carl Sagan's
sweatered biceps. Think of his barrel-chested
nerdy enthusiasm, his stringy black bangs
falling forward as he works out the math
for the surface temperature of Venus.

"Fred Ott's Sneeze"

Once, when I was a teenager, I caught
a man bending over in a long string

of sneezes. An older woman leaned close
and said, *You can always tell how a man*

will be in bed by how he sneezes.
After that, I couldn't help myself:

I'd think: *he makes that exact expression
when he comes.* I'd never waste my time

talking to any man who suppressed his sneezes.
One of the earliest motion pictures

made for the Edison Kinetoscope showed
a man take a pinch of snuff,

and the resulting sneeze. You'd watch it
through a peephole: 81 frames

of involuntary bodily contortions.
Seen in slow motion, it appears that Fred Ott

has a religious revelation:
beatitude, oblivion, explosion.

People paid to see this:
they called it *entertainment*.

Sucker Rods

Every time I drive to LAX
There's that field I look for

on the edge of the highway,
with all the oil rigs.

The land there's parched
and brown, as if it could never

yield a thing. A couple dozen
sucker rod pumps tick-tock,

the walking beams rock,
and at one end the weight

they call the horse's head
nods in rhythm

as it converts the rotary motion
of the beam into the linear motion

of the rods. The unhurried pace,
the syncopated upstroke:

it's a classic design, largely unchanged
from the 1920s, when it was first made,

when the great American thirst
really got started.

The Bluebonnet Carries 2,000 Amps

Who designed this system? Wires
suspended from high voltage
transmission towers

are made from twisted strands
of aluminum called conductors,
with standard sizes named

for flowers: *snapdragon, lupine,
valerian, narcissus*. Oh—don't forget
sneezewort. Some electrician

imagined a meadow hanging
thirty feet off the ground,
blossoming in air.

This is the kind of detail
a layperson calls *poetic*.
But no one thinks a line

of lattice-steel towers is pretty.
Erector-Set behemoths
straddle a strip-mowed hill

or march beside a highway,
conductors strung under their broad
shoulders, humming a bass note

in high winds, or flashing
ghostly coronas in the fog.
They look stark and industrial.

No one gets romantic
about 60 hertz
of alternating current.

No one really sings the body electric
or wanders magnetic fields
of amps, volts, ohms, watts.

Unless it's an electrician,
nostalgic for wild flowers.
Something with no power at all.

The Cardiff Giant

There were giants in the earth in those days.
The Cardiff Giant, 10 feet, 4 1/2 inches,
buried underground, petrified,
found in upstate New York in 1869
when Stub Newell hired men
to dig him a new well. Soon he had a tent instead,
and charged admission, and crowds
gathered to see the fossilized man
who proved Genesis 6:4. Newell sold him
to a man in Syracuse who moved him
with a crane, 2,900 pounds.
And even after the Yale paleontologist
pointed out the chisel marks and called the Giant
a hoax and a humbug, people still paid.
Barnum offered $60,000, was refused,
and made his own wax replica.
The owner of the true fake sued Barnum,
who countersued, and other fake fakes
were manufactured so the Giant could tour,
and giants walked the earth again.

The News

                In the morning, the sun paints Venetian stripes
      on my bedroom wall. When a cloud passes,

the pattern fades then returns, a camera
        going in and out of focus. The brighter the sun,
                the darker the shade: that's what I like best.

    That, and the way we are unable to stop
the stream of information
               we open our eyes to each morning, turning toward
the nightstand to read the big and little hands,

        waiting for the pattern of stripes to tell us,
                as if we were fish turning upstream
        and opening the pages of our daily gills,
what kind of life lies waiting.

II.

Hatchery

Hundreds of tiny fry
crowd the single tank,
churning the water milky.
The fry grow to parr
with wobbly, thick black stripes

as if drawn in a child's hand.
The parr grow to smolts,
released into ponds.
As they smoltify,
they turn silver, grow scales.

Their ponds go saline
and they grow, they fatten.
They bulk up, fish up,
they chinook, they chum,
they coho, they sockeye.

They don't run, or redd,
or spawn, or kelt.
No ocean, no river,
no homing. No anadromy.
They don't properly pink

so far from habitat.
So they're fed a food
made from themselves;
they are cannibalized
for color: soylent salmon.

And they are fed twice
as many pounds as they grow—
a crazy economy.
Still they are created
in the thousands, packed

into writhing tanks *like shooting fish
in a barrel.* Three years
from artificial insemination
to the flap of a caudal fin,
to the bagel on my plate.

A Boy Named Schmutz

His mother dressed him up so fine,
spent all her cash on sailor suits,
wool knickers with the sewn-in pleats,
and floppy grosgrain ribbon ties.
The Coney Island crowd of boys
liked him though: his dirty jokes,

his pitching arm. Also the way
he *let* his mother dress him up,
then watched her face go purple-red
screaming down the tenement walls
to all the ragged neighbor boys
who called him out to stickball games.

His name is Irving! she would shout
to my father and his gang below.
It's Irving! You dirty indigents!
You impecunious gutter rats!
No one screamed as gloriously:
How dare you beggars call him Schmutz!

In the Village

Too many birds to feed.
In Poland, in Lithuania,
black birds haunt the graveyards
where peasants once placed millet
to placate the winged dead.
But these birds come with questions
and the mouths of the peasants
have sealed firm as a flat horizon.
Black wings wheel overhead,
cover the rooftops,
their rusty voices ring through the square.
Too many blackbirds.
They cast shadows in the day
and at night, they block the stars.

Vilna

Celebrated as the capital of Yiddish literature.
Even the name of the city's different now,
but surely the River Neris still flows,
surely the brilliant stars still gather
above Mickiewicz Street, no matter
its current moniker. The dead hover
like some low-lying fog, even
though grandpa always said *the planet
turns only in one direction*. He meant:
don't drag old shadows into the new
country. Even if you carry Vilna
like an extra organ inside your chest.

Radiolaria

Ernst Haeckel, I can picture you
leaning over your microscope,
left eye closed, the right
open to one-celled worlds
where the quick and the still
yield their secrets.

The miraculous ocean
has entered the scope,
surged through your soul
and is now radiating out
the tips of your fingers,
which grasp a pencil

as you try to capture nature's
art, your *Kunstformen*.
The marine protozoa
called radiolaria convinced you
Darwin was right,
and your drawings persuaded

all of Europe.
There you are leaning late
with your amazing radiolaria
shaped like snowflakes and spiked crowns,
chandeliers and lobed planets.
This one branches like a crystal.

This one is a net of round holes
so dense it is as much absence
as physical shape. Note the symmetry
of the outstretched arms.
Miniature sunflower, butterfly,
apron, grid, I cannot

get enough of them. Look
at this elaborate helmet
with its quills and its spire.
Ernst Haeckel,
you turned out to be
a racist, an anti-Semite,

to believe in eugenics;
you created your own religion,
the Monist League,
and proclaimed a "crystal soul."
With all your rigor and your beauty,
your fine precision—I see you,

drawing that surprising jewel box
whose inner sanctum,
held in perfect equipoise
by its myriad winding tendrils,
contains nothing but darkness
and the infinite realms of cruelty.

The Vital Force

We have neither hooked beaks
like rapacious birds,
nor laddered lungs
by which a soul may climb.
No soft sounds to charm our ears
are heard beneath the waves.

We have neither fangs
like greedy wolves,
nor caustic spleen
by which a soul sets chase.
We may follow the threads
that Fortune spins,
but we can't destroy them.

Stentorious crackles,
tympanic echoes, issue
from the body's dark grottoes.
We have neither claws
like raging tigers,
nor the petalled liver,
a whorl of bilious burgundy
through which a soul is sluiced.

Either, like the smallest capillary,
the soul is vassal to the overlord heart.
Or the soul travels
the crankish, ornate maze
deep into the sumptuous
grey folds of the motile brain
and there is furnished,
and there is succored.

Sabbath

Do you see the miraculous carob tree
grow inside the cave? On this day,

Heart, honor your treaties;
Hearth, cease your labor.

Quiet all our pockets. Give no complaints
and make no petitions.

If the sky opens, build nothing,
let no unholy umbrellas intervene.

There is only a hat, so hold it high.
There are only the rules, a few blocks from home to *shul*

sanctified with string, and two white loaves.
That is your rest. That is your wellspring.

Campaign Speech, 1896:
"The Scourge of Foreign Elements"

The civilizing effects of modernity
have not yet smoothed the rough edges
of rummies, watch-stuffers, prostitutes

or thimble-riggers. Those who inflate
prices, tip scales, extort or confuse,
bring decay and imbecility, scandal and reproach.

We can no longer tolerate barefaced jobbery.
Citizens, lend your indignation to the cause.
The civilizing effects of modernity

demand the placement of public interests
where they properly belong, in the ameliorating
hands of authority. When vigilance

against sharks is allowed to weaken,
the poor are exposed in a forlorn, helpless
condition. Agents of bawdy-houses and thieves

make their harvest on the hapless,
who are strangers to our moral crusade
and the civilizing effects of modernity.

Selenium

Element 34 on the Periodic Table,
a Swede gave it the Greek name
      for the moon.

In glassmaking, it turns what's clear
to red, proving the moon is more
      than silver.

It occurs in nuts and fish,
most strongly in the Brazil nut,
      proving that Brazil

is a moonscape and Portuguese
the most lunatic tongue.
      When burned

it smells just like horseradish,
proving we Jews are the moon's
      natural population,

since we seek out the sharp
and the spicy, and like to cry
      when we eat

our fish and our nuts, and after
we are full and satisfied,
      we murmur softly

like waves lapping the shores
of the distant
      lunar beaches.

Burbot
lota lota

The burbot is a long thin fish.
Todd calls it an *eelpout* and curses its name;
it steals the bait he intends for walleyes,
it wraps around his arm when he releases
the hook, its teeth are numerous and sharp,

and its beard, the single barbel, odd.
He curses it and throws it back.
The French call it *river cod*
and poach the liver in white wine and make pâté
called *foix de lotte de rivière*. Alaskans

call it *ling cod* and bake it whole; chefs prize
its flakes of tender white flesh.
I've never tasted the fish.
Todd shows me photos on his phone:
he wants to brag about his tricked-out

ice-fishing shack with its large-screen TV
and all the walleyes he catches.
Everyone in Wisconsin, he insists,
hates the eelpout. Turns out it's the only
freshwater fish in the cod family.

Was it separated from its salty kin
by continental shift, by some early
unmarked cataclysm? The burbot is the only
freshwater fish to spawn in winter,
at the same time as saltwater cod.

Burbots rise each winter from the depths
for a shallow orgy, sometimes a hundred or more
intertwined bodies in a quivering ball,
releasing eggs and sperm, churning
beneath a blanket of ice.

Life in Connecticut, October 1704: From the Journal of Sarah Kemble Knight

Oysters in great plenty line the coast.
They generally live well and comfortably.
But too indulgent—farmers are the worst—

to slaves. It is enough to bond their trust,
but *suff'ring great familiarity*
like oysters bed together? It will cost,

permitting slaves *to sit at Table just
(as they say) to save time.* This Colony
is too indulgent. Ye farmers much the worst,

not knowing in what leniency is lost.
Into the dish there goes the black hoof freely,
oysters in great plenty not the least,

as freely as the white hand. Where I lodged
I was received with all Civility,
but too indulgent. Farmers are the worst,

though *lacking not in Mother Wit.* I rest
after so long and toilsome a journey,
eat oysters in too much plenty from the coast,
indulge my crowded mind to sow my worst.

I am the Pâtissier of God

"I am the punishment of God." –Genghis Khan

I am the pâtissier of God.
If you had not committed great sins,
God would not have set a pâtissier
like me upon you. On the banks
of Amu Darya, all sugar tastes extra sweet.
The country is choked with halvah
and the air cloys like uzvar
but whoever yields and submits
to shirinlik is free from the disgrace
of its severity. Turkic defenders
flee before my pastry. Among you
are those who withhold
out of greed: it is not hunger
that will be your undoing. Shakarli
will be spread out in front of you
and you will vie for it
as if transformed into a giant sweet tooth,
and it will destroy you.

Turkey in the Straw

This must have been in 1991,
when all the city's central neighborhoods
were boarded up. Parades of prostitutes
in hot pants and high heels roamed Logan Circle
and we were named the Murder Capital.
Lying in my bed at night I'd hear
the alleys echo gunfire. Every day
a truck jangled through my neighborhood,
and sometimes parked for hours on my block.
The smiling clowns, the painted popsicles
the vendor didn't sell: rocket pops,
big dippers, cookie-wiches.
No. Everybody knew the crack truck,
brazen with its blaring happy chimes
that loop-de-looped to "Turkey in the Straw"—
a siren's call to shipwreck young men's boats.

Hearing Loss

1.

Hammer, anvil, and stirrup
furnish the yellow vestibule,
echo every faint breeze,
rustle of paper, small words
long forgotten, spoken close and low.
Long after the electric pulses,
the reverberation slows:
this is song.
The vibration lingers, white bones
that shiver and buzz; the room
is not empty. Here is the drum,
the cilia, the perfect alignments.
Here the desire.
Here the memory of desire.

2.

Hear the memory of desire:
rustle of paper, small words
that shiver and buzz, the room
long forgotten, spoken close and low.
The vibration lingers in white bones—
hammer, anvil, and stirrup—
furnished. The yellow vestibule
is not empty. Here, the drum,
the cilia. The perfect alignments
slow the reverberation:
long after the electric pulses
echoed every faint breeze,
here was desire.
This was song.

Six

The number of feet to dig for a coffin.
The highest roll of the die.
The symbol of Venus, goddess of love.
The atomic number of carbon.
As a prefix, either *hex* or *sex*.
A group of French composers in the 1920s.

The crystal structure of ice.
Equal to the telephone's M, N and O.
A senator's term of office.
A bright red stop sign.
The most efficient shape for circuits.
The waxy architecture of the honeycomb.

The smallest positive integer
that is neither a square number
or a prime number.
The age I started the first grade.
The number of points on a Star of David.
The number of days it took to create the world.

The Immovable Empyrean

> *"...it has come to this, that a dead man was then of no more account than a dead goat would be today."* —*Giovanni Boccaccio,* The Decameron

Mercury makes men ambitious for glory.
Saturn makes men temperate as monks.
The gates of the ghetto were locked at dusk,
unlocked at dawn, until the plague
washed over the city, and we Jews
were barred inside. Food was scarce
and clean water even more rare.

But buboes were plentiful, as big as eggs
in the armpits, as big as apples
in the groin, the stench venting
when lanced by a doctor.
The gates were fortified
with wooden stockades; the healthy
knew the only release was death.

Some said the air was corrupted
with putrid vapors that stuck to clothes
and entered the body, the arcadian body,
through pores in the skin.
Some bathed in vinegar. Some
burned tar to cleanse the air.
Some thought even talk was toxic.

Astronomers blamed the conjunction
of aggressive Mars
and humid Jupiter, the planets moving
in a black labyrinth of space,
the immovable empyrean.
When red carbuncles appeared on the torso,
it was only a matter of days, perhaps hours.

Under the lens, the bacteria, *Yersina pestis*,
is shaped like rods. Its vector is blood,
its strategy is multiplication.
The language of disease is mathematics:
the black labyrinth of the body,
the internal maze of vessels,
capillary, vein, artery, aorta, heart.

The International Fruit of Welcome

A pineapple is the perfect gift
to bring to a blind date.
A pineapple is like a blind date:
spiky and armored at first,
with the hope of sweetness inside.
A pineapple is the perfect housewarming gift.
You don't have to wrap it,
it doesn't spill inside your car.
It comes in its own house.
A pineapple is the perfect birthday gift.
You might prefer a coconut,
that planet molten at the core,
but the pineapple has a better hairdo,
better wardrobe; it never
goes out of style.
Think of all those historic houses
with pineapple bolsters, pineapple finials,
pineapples carved above lintels.
Such a sophisticated fruit:
every sailor wants one.

III.

Swamp

The Lincoln sinks into the Potomac
with a sigh. Constitution Avenue,
weary of constraint, reverts to canal,
complete with stink and Spring floods.

Swamp reclaims the grounds
of the Washington Monument, and river
reclaims the rest, filling with masts
that glided in from the Chesapeake Bay.

All the mere human efforts
of the Army Corps of Engineers
have come to naught. The Kennedy Center's
massive bunker, like a Soviet tank, slides

under the gurgling mud and the bridges dissolve,
their long lines of cars a dim specter.
Across the wide dirt roads downtown
Walt Whitman strides in his boots,

kicking up clouds of dust that eddy in his wake
—until he, too, wavers and melts
amid white columned buildings,
and the classical ruins of grand intent.

Sonnet for the U.S. Capitol Dome

Driving down North Cap some afternoons
that vista looks so fake, a cardboard dome
pasted on a summer album's page.
When Congress is in session, winter nights
they light the topknot, called the lantern—bright
and merry as a party. Dante wrote:
"Cut off from hope, we go on in desire."
Picabia once said, "The head is round
so thoughts can change direction." Every Fall,
a plague of crows like freshmen senators
ascends the Hill in dancing shrouds. They roost
among a palisade of narrow spikes
placed evenly amid the cast iron ribs,
and oil their squeaky wings for a new season.

Presidential Rondeaux

1. Rondeau Beginning with a Quote from John Adams

I read my eyes out and can't read half enough.
My ears are leaking fine gray matter fluff.
My fingers have been flayed down to the bone.
My Sahara-throat just manages a groan.
Books have left me stripped down to the buff.

From "mother's womb, untimely ripped" Macduff
can slay the king, made worthy through his suff-
ering. That's a book for you! All alone,
I read my eyes out.

My lungs from lack of exercise can't puff,
my skin's albino alligator rough
but still with book in hand I lie here prone
and I'll continue till a shriveled crone.
No greater privilege—no!—no greater love:
to read my eyes out.

2. Rondeau Beginning with a Quote from Lyndon Baines Johnson

You ain't learning nothin' when you're talking.
A tile's useless when it lacks good caulking.
Although the craftsman owns the proper tool,
that doesn't save his art from ridicule:
a telescope don't make you Stephen Hawking.

Time doesn't slow when you neglect your clocking;
Diane von Fürstenberg has finished frocking.
You're waiting in some slack-jawed vestibule
and you ain't learning nothin'.

A ship is still a vessel in dry-docking.
Velour is valued by its depth of flocking.
When reciprocity's the golden rule,
as Schopenhauer warns us, "fate is cruel."
On the Great Blackboard, we are merely chalking,
and you ain't learning nothin'.

E Pluribus Unum

His false teeth.
His wife's sheets
hanging in the East
Room. His walls of snaking
brick. His wife saving
portraits from the fire.
His good feelings,
his long trousers,
his coon-skin attire.
His silver goblet and golden plate.
His sudden death
after hours hatless in cold rain.
Alas, alas:
his many progeny,
his manifest destiny,
his horse, Whitey,
grazing on the White House grass.

Quebec Place NW, Park View Neighborhood

"See the new Kennedy Homes. Remarkable values for the price. Eight rooms, finished in oak and mahogany. Overlooking prettiest part of Solder's Home Park."
–Washington Post *advertisement, 1917*

A two-block strip of road ends with a view
between black iron bars of an expanse
of sculpted green we're not invited to.

A hundred years exactly have elapsed
since these two-story houses with their porches
leapt in three dimensions from their plans:

solid brick, gas lighting, attic dormers,
ice box, indoor plumbing, a garage
special-built for autos, not for horses.

A streetcar ride away from downtown jobs
but at an open, healthy elevation:
a neighborhood built to defy the odds

of Federal clerks with backbone and ambition.
On summer nights they'd pour in through the gate
(before these houses became air-conditioned),

a blanket staking out each family's place
on the cooler grasses of the Soldier's Home
to eat their picnic dinners, stay up late,

then in safekeeping of the distant dome
of the Capitol in fading purple light,
they fell asleep in tousled knots, still clothed,

women in their crinolines and tights,
in corsets. One communal sleep: how brave!
Who would choose that now on summer nights?

The Park Road Gate, in 1955,
was closed off. At some later unknown year,
they topped the iron fences with barbed wire.

After Hours in the Kindergarten

It's geography week at school.
The kindergarten halls are lined
with identical pictures: Mrs. Benton's
penguins, repeated blobs in black and white.

I move out of the polar regions.
What is that odd smell hiding beneath
disinfectant? On a low table I find
white styrofoam painted mud-brown,

notched rectangles that once enclosed
computer components, now glued
in a standing row, topped with toilet paper rolls,
also painted, topped with little paper

Chinese flags, yellow stars on red.
Why, it's the Great Wall of China!
Styrofoam walls, cardboard watch towers
—I kneel to look closely—

one of the wonders of the world,
here between the girl's bathroom
and the janitor's closet,
fantastic in fluorescent light.

Double Indemnity

No, not insurance. What I
meant to say was "double identity,"

as in Boutros Boutros-Ghali,
William Carlos Williams, Sirhan Sirhan,

Lady Gaga. For these folks, surely,
The Postman Always Rings Twice.

But now I've Mildred Pierced myself
to the image of James M. Cain,

typing away in his little white house
in suburban Maryland. His typewriter

is preserved in a university library;
I've seen it. I've seen the change

from manual to electric to electronic
to what-the-hell-is-a-typewriter

and no one will be archiving
our battered beloved i-Pads,

even if they once belonged to Yo Yo Ma,
Flava Flav, or Marky Mark.

Now all our devices must do at least
two things: phone-cameras,

calculator-umbrellas. But in truth
all of us lead double lives, an outer

story plus a hidden story, separated by
such a thin skin. Tell us that one again

Ford Madox Ford, Kris Kristofferson,
Humbert Humbert, Richie Rich.

Extreme Makeover: The Home Edition

On television, giant backhoes push
a house apart. The walls collapse; the roof's
a jaunty cap atop the ruins. Our host,
Ty Pennington, milks the tragedy:
the father's dying wish, the mother's tears,
the stoic courage of the little son
born with some rare, untreatable disease.
Goodbye to faulty wiring, toxic mold,
the flooding basement, dead appliances.
They scrape and grade the lot, pour concrete in
the new foundations, hoist frames into place.
At three times larger than the old, this house
will sport a dozen bathrooms and a pool,
a shiny silver kitchen straight from Sears.
Each week, another family's stunned surprise,
the mortgage paid in full, the new Ford van.
And even though the stories start to meld,
I watch each week, addicted, from my couch,
this myth of starting over, scraping clean
to bedrock. *Do it: call the backhoes in.*

Photo with Woman at Clothes Line

Drawn to them as if subpoenaed
to give her life to the horizontal,
the ever moving, the innumerable vertical

with its sad expectancy and ignorance
driving its legendary ribs of wind;
compelled by their intricate logic,

their proud barrier stance, she bowed
to their recommendation, hugged
the curve of their deserted houses,

their brittle dependency to weather,
to changes in the air—shirts and coveralls,
dresses and sheets—neighbored,

landscaped, holding immense and empty hands
and waiting, lined up for her blessing,
her obsession, her worship which would

transfigure, her beautiful and necessary
tunnel of devotion to a ship of air:
to the mere, to the daily, to the glorious mundane.

Thirteen Ways of Looking at DC Not Endorsed by the Tourist Board: A Poem in the Subjunctive Mood Without Any Cloture

If this city were an instrument,
it would be a sousaphone.
Each August, seeds fall from lotus pods
shaped like shower heads
into a series of artificial ponds.
And all the shallow plastic cups
of mambo sauce in all the corner takeouts
can't make up for the thin shadow
our Shadow Senator casts.
If this city were a building,
it would be a triangular low-rise
cut on a sharp diagonal plane.
In a single April weekend,
all the Yoshino cherry trees
unclench their branches
and weep soft pink coins.
We have a Darth Vader gargoyle,
and coffered subway ceilings
of cast concrete honeycombs.
Filibuster is not named
for some Senator Phil. It's a bastardized
Dutch word for *freebooter* or *pirate*.
If this city were a forecast, it would be
high humidity for yet another week.
It would be discovered
in a rented hotel room yelling
Bitch set me up.

Mystery Piano in the Woods

A light snow was falling
but the piano was still in perfect tune:
an upright in a grove of maple and beech,
its obedient wooden bench trailing,
intact, without scars, as if the piano
had merely stepped out of its parlor
to sniff the air, to look at the cloud cover,
the way we might step off our porches
without a coat, just for a minute.
No sheet music, no rap sheet;
no one reported it missing.
One police officer remembered enough
from childhood lessons to try
a harmonic minor scale
and reported its action was excellent.
For two weeks straight, the officer
couldn't shake the image;
he dreamed of if every single night:
a dissident piano waltzing in the woods
to Chopin's Revolutionary Etude
under a fresh insurrection of snow.

The Garden of Ryoan-Ji

> *"Before enlightenment, mountains are mountains and waters are waters."* —Qingyuan Weixin

Water-cutting stone, shadow-facing stone,
stone of the spirit-king, demon stone,
stone of the two-fold world.

In a garden of stones, one stone
sings. One stone fishes for stones
with a stone lure. And one stone
swims among the stones wearing
stony scales, grey with small flashes
of mica. One stone
floats on its back and impersonates
a cumulus cloud.

Hovering mist stone,
torso stone, lying sideways stone.
One stone stops singing
to listen for its echo.

The Shipwreck

Painted in 1805, part of a retrospective of the works of J.M.W. Turner exhibited at the National Gallery of Art, Washington DC

In Turner's painting *The Shipwreck*
everything leans and moans,

even the glowering clouds.
Three small wooden craft

are flung from the drowning ship.
The striped cap of the sailor at the tiller

looks like exposed ribs,
while in the other life boats

men drape agonized atop one another
and waves hoist

their hummocks of foam.
The young genius, the painter,

lingers lovingly, reaching
over each violent wrench of water.

The Shipwreck is his first large-scale oil,
his palettes and knives and brushes reaching,

desperate, through a vortex of small men
centered on their unfolding disaster,

two dozen hopeless figures
hemmed in by a dense black sky.

The Suicide of Clover Adams

I. *The Adams Memorial by Augustus Saint-Gaudens, Rock Creek Cemetery*

The crunch of gravel, thickly laid,
the cool marble of the bench,
inside a box of dense boxwood,
framing its hexagon of sky.

The cool marble of the bench
pressed against my tender thighs
frames its hexagon. The sky,
like the stone, reveals no names.

Pressed against my chilling thighs
I lean forward, toward the figure—
she reveals no names,
no secrets. In heavy drape

she leans forward too: a figure hooded,
her face serene, inscrutable.
Her secrets are heavily draped
in enclosing bronze cloth,

her face serene, unreadable.
The crunch of gravel, thickly laid,
like her enclosing bronze cloth,
remains hidden inside its box of boxwood.

II. *Tea with the Five of Hearts*

Her sharp tongue made her "unfashionable."
Her sharp eye gave her photographs
a detailed intimacy. High tea
was open to just a loyal few.

Her sharp eye permeated her photographs,
Japanese prints, low-slung armchairs
enjoyed by only a loyal few,
her china hand-painted with the five of hearts.

Those Japanese prints and low-slung armchairs—
a sensibility quite modern—
china hand-painted with the five of hearts
(an inside joke). And Henry grumpy:

his sensitivity. Quite modern,
how she teased him out
with inside jokes. Henry was always grumpy
and she, curious, full of wonder.

How she teased him out
with her sharp tongue, her unfashionable
curiosity. No wonder
her high tea was a detailed intimacy.

III. *The Darkroom*

In the end, it was not enough.
Six servants, two horses, three dogs—
too much to manage. And Henry,
with those dead presidents in the family.

Six servants, two horses, three dogs—
all reported in a weekly letter to her dear papa.
With these presidents in the family
staring at her across Lafayette Square,

she reported in her papa's Sunday letter,
it was like serving her tea to ghosts.
Staring across Lafayette Square
or in the sweet retreat of her darkroom

she served her ghosts. Mixing the tea
of chemicals, that acrid toxic tang
in the sweet retreat of her darkroom,
ferric acid, silver bromide, potassium cyanide.

The chemicals, that acrid toxic tang:
in the end it was quite enough.
Ferric acid, silver bromide, potassium cyanide—
so much to swallow. And Henry.

Half-Built House

Does love reside in the body? No heart is heart-shaped.

No star is star-shaped. And none have currency. By the time light travels such distance, it's already spent.

These mistakes go on and on. Misconceptions sown in the body. A new house is best when it is half-built, and you have to imagine the walls.

Sometimes inchoate things shine brightest. I think love is locked in the heart of the house, how we played at living there, inhabiting outlines, touching the frame.

Van Gogh at Arles

Twelve simple chairs of blond wood with rush seats in a yellow house in the yellow light slanting in from the south. Twelve chairs like twelve disciples in *the vigorous sun, like sulfur*.

One larger dark chair, waiting for Gauguin. The master's chair—and in his bedroom, sunflowers.

The plain of the Crau, the ancient cemetery, the women with their classical Roman profiles, poplars, twelve rush-bottomed chairs, a crate of onions.

Working *de tête* didn't suit him. He was made for the *étude*, quick strokes taken from nature, *accidents in pigment* that shimmer.

But the mistral blew out the sun and forced everyone indoors. Green shutters knocking against the sides of the yellow house. The *Arlésiennes* pulling their dark shawls over their heads, clasping the wool tight at their chins.

A self-portrait: the spartan chair is seen from above, as from a great height. It looks hopeful, on a simple tile floor. Yellow, his color, but outlined in blue.

Be responsive to the object: to line and color. Style is more important than deliberate composition. *It does me good to do difficult things.*

The Glass Flowers at Harvard

*Created by Leopold and Rudolph Blaschka, Bohemian
glassmakers and jewelers, between 1886 and 1936*

The transverse section of a water lily ovary
is delicate and ornate as a snowflake
but tinged cerulean at the outer edges.

Individual balls of pollen with spikes
are magnified to enormous sizes
and resemble translucent blowfish.

Wool sower galls from a white oak,
quercus alba, the growths partially cut away,
form around a glass wasp.

Lilies in bloom have root systems
tangled as a knot of Gorgon hair.
Goldenrod crowds its tiny lobed florets.

Nutmeg stems bow low under the weight
of heavy, waxy, yellow fruit.
Button-wood, witch hazel,

the ratchety stalk of the small-flowered
Agrimony. The leggy Lord Anson's
Blue Pea has wiry corkscrews

at the ends of each leaf stalk.
The cashew fruit has puppet heads.
A maple leaf in autumn hues wears a red-orange

it took the Blaschkas a decade to perfect.
After the father died, the son continued on
alone. Over 800 plant species, flame worked,

enameled in a wash of metal oxide.
The wetlands weed known as Floating Heart,
Pigeon-berry, also known as Sky Flower,

4,400 models in all, forever blooming.
Laid out in rows of wooden cases,
a life's work, glass under glass.

American Herring Gull

>*Down from the shower'd halo,*
>*Up from the mystic play of shadows twining and twisting as if they were alive,*
>*Out from the patches of briers and blackberries,*
>*From the memories of the bird that chanted to me..."*
>   —From "Out of the Cradle Endlessly Rocking" by Walt Whitman

Beneath a lazy whiptail of cloud,
Beneath that flimsy arc of white,
Under an eighth-month moon,
Where the strand arcs too in a mirror of sky
And each particle of sand grips inward tight and fetal
Inside its hard heart, granite and yellow,
Where the waves arch their backs and collapse,
Where the waves inhale then collapse,
And the wet curve is laid low,
Down from the shower'd halo,

Up from the white foam receding,
Or not receding, leaving its fallen petals on the beach,
Flimsy whiptail cloud-like arcs
Under the wing of a gull hunting her tidbits,
Surveying her beach kingdom, sea lettuce, limpet, moon shell,
Where any tinfoil glint brings her swoop and dive,
Where any updraft pulls her inland
Over fleabane and wax myrtle, over sumac,
Up where the air is cooler, where the wind quickens and revives,
Up from the mystic play of shadows twining and twisting as if they were alive,

Away from the gnarled, earthbound complexities,
The thickets of hurt feelings
And the petty sparring of fashion;
Up from the hardpan where every foot is muffled
As if of no consequence, of no history,

She lifts her white wings, slightly tarnished, and carries
Under her hanging pink feet a windfall,
An earthly tidbit brought high and clear
To that place above the gridlock and worries,
Out from the patches of briers and blackberries

Above the North Atlantic Drift,
Above the hard stretch of yellow sand, the woman
Walking alone there, following the rick-rack of the tide-line,
following the gentle curve of the shore,
But not really alone, no, beachcombing for something unnamed
Something just out of reach
But part of her—I should say part of me, my doppelganger,
The shadow discipled to my transmuted self,
Out of the salty, amniotic sea,
From the memories of the bird that chanted to me...

Notes

"The Scientific Method"
Dedicated to Susan Boscarino.
In addition to the Chemistry Lab and Stockroom mentioned here, the Edison Laboratory Complex holds: a heavy machine shop, precision machine shop, drafting room, music recording studio, photography department, metallurgical lab, physics lab, Room 5 (the experimental lab), and an ornate two-story library. Now run by the National Park Service, the site exhibits an amazing array of original equipment and materials. Two men really were stuck inside the labs for three whole days during the Blizzard of 1888, and survived by eating "the more appetizing" stockroom supplies; their names were Reginald Fessenden and Jonas Aylsworth. I took the liberty of shortening Alysworth's last name.

"The Thing in the Thing"
Dedicated to Gwen Rubinstein.

"The Invasive Weed Syndicate"
Dedicated to my allergist, Dr. Nirupma Rohatgi.

"Fowler and Wells' Phrenological Cabinet"
Lorenzo and Orson Fowler were the foremost American proponents of a pseudo-scientific craze in the mid-19th century, to "read" the bumps on a person's skull and determine a sitter's natural propensities, both positive and negative. Participants could then use this information to improve aspects of their personality and work toward "perfectibility of the soul." The Fowlers published the *American Phrenological Journal*, as well as Whitman's second edition of *Leaves of Grass*. They ran an office in New York City from 1834 to 1863, and in Boston from 1863 to 1880.

"The Moon and *The Sun*"
When Sir John Herschel (1792 - 1871), the English mathematician and astronomer, first heard of the Great Moon Hoax, he expressed amusement, noting that his real observations could never compete in excitement. But in later years, as journalists continued to pester him with questions, he got increasingly annoyed about the mis-use of his name.

"Walt Whitman's Brain"
The American Anthropometric Society was founded in 1889, and dedicated to the study of the human brain. A membership report from 1906 related: "The brain of Walt Whitman, together with the jar in which it had been placed, was said to have been dropped upon the floor through carelessness in handling. Unfortunately, not even the pieces were saved."

"Building the Perhapsitron"
This poem is based on phrases lifted from "A Star in a Bottle" by Raffi Khatchadourian, published in *The New Yorker*, March 3, 2014. The "he" of the poem is actually a composite of several scientists who have worked on fusion experiments.

"Carl Sagan's Turtleneck Sweater"
Dedicated to Dan Vera.

"The Cardiff Giant"
George Hull, an atheist and a tobacconist by trade, ordered a block of gypsum from Iowa, hired Edward Burghart to sculpt it, then artificially aged the "petrified man" with a combination of stains, acids, and by flailing it with a board embedded with steel knitting needles. He then buried it at his cousin's farm in Cardiff, New York where he knew it would be discovered "accidentally" by workers. Hull spent $2,600 to create the Giant, but later sold it for $23,000—a tidy profit. The Giant is still on display; since 1947, it's been in the collections of the Farmers' Museum in Cooperstown, New York.

"A Boy Named Schmutz"
Schmutz is the Yiddish word for dirt. I know almost nothing about my taciturn father's childhood in Brooklyn; this is the one and only story I remember him telling.

"Radiolaria"
Ernst Haeckel (1834 – 1919) was a German biologist, physician, professor, and zoologist who discovered and named thousands of new species, and popularized Charles Darwin's theories in Germany. His detailed illustrations of animals and sea creatures are truly remarkable.

"Sabbath"
The carob tree image is a reference to a tale from the Midrash about Rabbi Shimon and his son, who, escaping persecution by the Romans, were able to live for 13 years in a cave because a miracle occurred: God created a carob tree and a wellspring of water for them. This poem refers to the rules that Orthodox Jews observe during the Sabbath. *Shul* is Yiddish for synagogue.

"Campaign Speech, 1896: The Scourge of Foreign Elements"
This poem borrows heavily from anti-Semitic and anti-immigrant language prevalent at the time my grandparents immigrated to the United States from what is today Lithuania.

"Selenium"
Selenium was discovered in 1817 by a Swedish chemist, Jöns Jacob Berzelius. I first became aware of its significance as a micronutrient after I began treatment for hypothyroidism, as selenium plays an important role in thyroid function.

"Life in Connecticut, October 1704: From the Journal of Sarah Kemble Knight"
Knight (1666 – 1727) was a business owner and teacher. The journal relates a courageous journey by horseback from Boston to New York City, during a time when roads were few, traveller's accommodations nonexistent, and women generally did not travel alone. The journal is notable for its humor, and its detailed record of early settlements in New England. Much as I enjoyed reading it, the single racist phrase I quote was the one thing that stuck most forcefully in my memory afterward, notable for its assumption that any educated reader of the diary would share her viewpoint. The journal was published posthumously in 1825, and the original manuscript has been lost, leading to some contention among scholars about its true authorship. In the summer of 2012, I tracked down Knight's grave at Ye Antientist Burial Ground in New London, CT, the town where she settled in later years with her daughter.

"I am the Pâtissier of God"
In 1218, when the Mongols invaded what is today Uzbekistan, they leveled the main cities of Samarkand and Bukhara. Genghis Khan is reputed to have climbed atop the pulpit in the great mosque of Bukhara,

where the remaining residents were gathered, to proclaim: "I am the punishment of God. If you had not committed great sins, God would not have sent a punishment like me."

"The International Fruit of Welcome"
Dedicated to Regie Cabico.

"Swamp"
Dedicated to Martin G. Murray.

"Presidential Rondeaux"
Dedicated to Michael Gushue.

"E Pluribus Unum"
This poem references, in order, an attribute or commonly known story for each of the first twelve U.S. Presidents.

"Quebec Place NW, Park View Neighborhood"
The park residents are viewing in the Park View neighborhood is the U.S. Armed Forces Retirement Home (colloquially known as the Old Soldier's Home), 272 acres of rolling green pasture, dotted with fishing ponds, winding paths, a nine-hole golf course, and statuary. Because it includes some of the highest ground in the city, it was considered defensively important during the Civil War as a lookout point; Abraham Lincoln used it as a "summer White House." After the assassination of Martin Luther King, Jr. and the subsequent riots in DC, the iron fence surrounding the property was topped with three rows of barbed wire crowned with concertina coils.

"Double Indemnity"
James M. Cain's papers and his manual typewriter are preserved in the special collections of the University of Maryland libraries. Cain (1892-1977), who helped develop the literary form we now called "hardboiled crime fiction," was a former journalist who lived in a modest frame house near the university from 1948 until his death. His novels include *The Postman Always Rings Twice* (1934), *Serenade* (1937), *Mildred Pierce* (1941), and *Double Indemnity* (1943).

"*Extreme Makeover: The Home Edition*"
The reality television show that provided home improvements for needy recipients (or more often simply knocked down older homes and replaced them) ran weekly on network TV from 2003 to 2012. Although highly formulaic, I found it addictive.

"Photo with Woman at Clothes Line"
In memory of my mother, Barbara Ellen Berwick Roberts (1936 – 2016).

"Thirteen Ways of Looking at DC Not Endorsed by the Tourist Board"
In memory of Marion Shepilov Barry, Jr. (1936 – 2014).
To those who are not DC insiders, some of the references here might need explaining. John Philip Sousa was a native son who conducted the U.S. Marine Band. He is best remembered as the composer of "Stars and Stripes Forever." He developed the sousaphone, a lighter-weight tuba, for use in marching bands. The lotus ponds mentioned are the Kenilworth Aquatic Gardens, the only national park devoted to water plants. Mambo sauce (also known as mumbo sauce) is a sweet, tangy barbecue sauce first popularized in DC in the 1960s and universally found in the city's takeout restaurants. As a district, not a state, DC residents have no representation in the U.S. Congress. We do, however, elect a Shadow Representative and a Shadow Senator to lobby for full voting rights. A gargoyle sculpted to look like Darth Vader, the villain of the "Star Wars" movies, really does exist on the northwest tower of the National Cathedral. When DC's longest-serving mayor, Marion Barry, was caught by the FBI in a hotel room with crack cocaine and a prostitute in 1990, he repeated "Bitch set me up" numerous times (as caught on videotape). This refrain became a catch-phrase used by locals to express a wide range of grievances.

"Mystery Piano in the Woods"
Based on a *New York Daily News* report, November 24, 2008: "Mystery piano, abandoned deep in the woods, baffles Cape Cod police."

"The Garden of Ryoan-ji"
Dedicated to Christina Daub.
Considered the finest surviving example of a dry landscape (*kare-sansui*) Zen garden, Ryoan-ji was built in the second half of the 15th century and is located at the Temple of the Dragon at Peace in Kyoto, Japan.

Qingyuan Weixin was an influential Zen scholar of the Tang Dynasty; the epigraph is from his most famous kōan. I fell in love with *kare-sansui* as a child, in frequent visits to the Chinese Garden Court at the Metropolitan Museum of Art in New York.

"The Shipwreck"
This early painting by Joseph Mallord William Turner was inspired by a poem by the same name by William Falconer, which recounts the final voyage of the merchant ship *Britannia*. The poet, who would (ironically) later die by shipwreck himself, wrote:

> *Again she plunges! Hark! A second shock*
> *Tears her strong bottom on the marble rock!*
> *Down on the vale of death, with dismal cries,*
> *The fated victims shuddering roll their eyes,*
> *In wild despair, while yet another stroke,*
> *With deep convulsion, rends the solid oak:*
> *Till like the mine, in whose infernal cell*
> *The lurking demons of destruction dwell…*

I became enamored of the idea of this subject coming full circle, of writing a poem on a painting based on a poem.

"The Suicide of Clover Adams"
Dedicated to Teri Ellen Cross Davis.
Marion Hooper Adams, known to friends as Clover, married the author and historian Henry Adams in 1872, and moved with him to DC. Clover came from a prominent and wealthy Boston family. She was clever, outspoken, with a dazzling wit and a sharp tongue. She wrote that Adams was "utterly devoted" to her. They were unable to have children, a great disappointment to both of them. The main character of Henry's novel *Democracy*, Madeleine Lee, seems to be inspired in part by Clover. Clover was also the model for Henry James's Mrs. Bonnycastle in his short story "Pandora." Always prone to depression, Clover was deeply struck by the death of her father in 1885. She committed suicide in a particularly gruesome way, in her home: she poisoned herself by drinking some of her photographic chemicals. She was 42 years old, and had been married for twelve years. The memorial Henry built for her (where he

was later interred himself) is a masterpiece of American figurative art. As per Henry Adams's instructions, it lists no names or dates. A favorite retreat for Eleanor Roosevelt, the memorial was written about by Mark Twain, John Galsworthy (in his novel *Two Forsyte Interludes*), Alexander Woollcott (who called it "the most beautiful thing ever fashioned by the hand of man on this continent"), and Anthony Hecht, among others. In 1972, it was added to the Register of Historic Places.

"The Glass Flowers at Harvard"
The Ware Collection of Glass Flowers is on display at the Harvard Museum of Natural History in Cambridge, MA. In Marianne Moore's poem "Silence" the narrator quotes her father saying:

> *"Superior people never make long visits,*
> *have to be shown Longfellow's grave*
> *nor the glass flowers at Harvard…"*

Superior people, I maintain, should make every effort to find their own way there. The models, commissioned by Professor George Lincoln Goodale, were used to teach botany. They are extraordinary.

Books by Kim Roberts

Poetry
The Scientific Method (2017)
Fortune's Favor: Scott in the Antarctic (2015)
Animal Magnetism (2011)
The Kimnama (2007)
The Wishbone Galaxy (1994)

Anthology
Full Moon on K Street: Poems About Washington, DC (2010)

Nonfiction
Lip Smack: A History of Spoken Word Poetry in DC (2010)

Kim Roberts lives in Washington, DC. She co-edits two literary journals, *Beltway Poetry Quarterly* and the *Delaware Poetry Review*. She is the recipient of grants from the National Endowment for the Humanities, Humanities DC, and the DC Commission on the Arts, as well as grants to be a writer-in-residence at 15 artist colonies. *The Scientific Method* is her fifth book of poems.

Printed in Great Britain
by Amazon